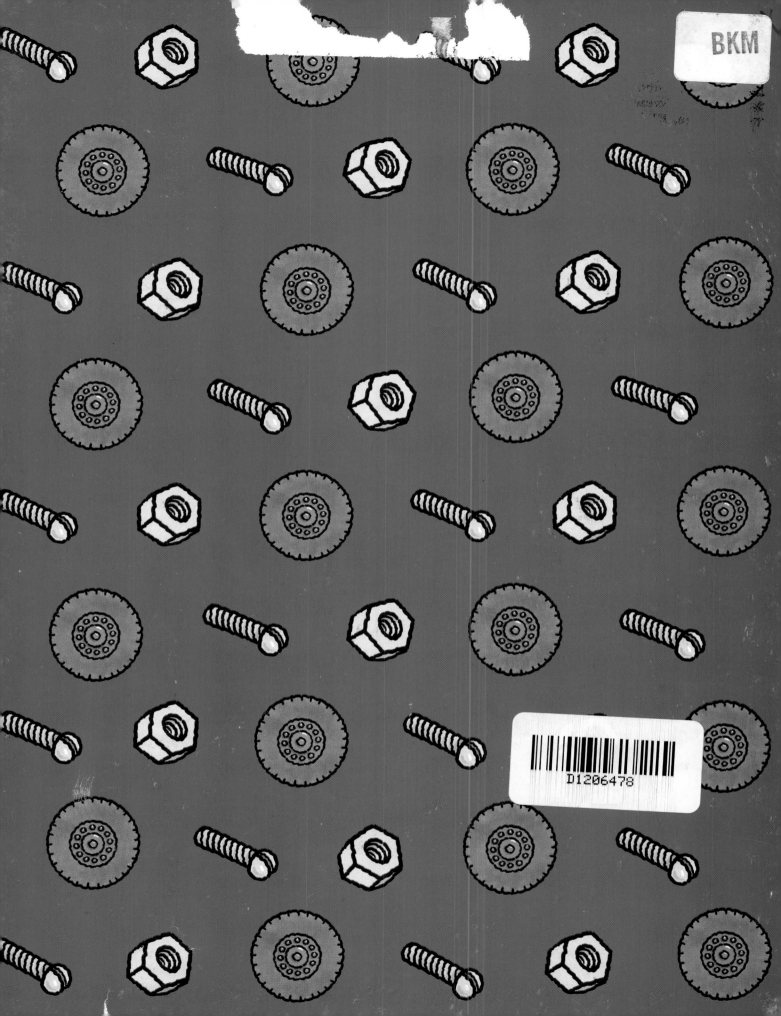

A DK PUBLISHING BOOK

Editor Mary Ling
Designer Claire Penny
Managing Editor Sheila Hanly
US Editor Camela Decaire
Production Josie Alabaster
Photography Richard Leeney
Illustrator Ellis Nadler
Picture research Ingrid Nilsson

First American edition, 1996
4 6 8 10 9 7 5 3

Published in the United States by
DK Publishing, Inc.,
95 Madison Avenue, New York, New York 10016

Copyright © 1996 Dorling Kindersley Limited, London

A CIP catalog record is available from the
Library of Congress.
ISBN: 0-7894-0575-X

Color reproduction by Chromagraphics, Singapore
Printed and bound in Italy by L.E.G.O.

DK would like to thank: Ainscough Crane Hire Ltd,
Lancs; British Aerospace Airbus Ltd. Chester; Halls
Automotive, Kent; Redland Readymix, Darlington;
WSM, Bristol for allowing their vehicles to be
photographed and for all their help and advice.

The publisher would like to thank the following for their
kind permission to reproduce their photographs:
l left, r right, t top, c center, b below
C Bingham 19tr; Robert Harding Picture Library 5br,
18/19c; Image Bank 8; Syndicated Truck Features/Steve
Sturgess 4/5c, 6/7bl; Telegraph Colour Library/
Masterfile 4bc, 9tr; S Windsor 9bl.

Every effort has been made to trace the copyright
holders and we apologize in advance for any
unintentional omissions. We would be pleased to
insert the appropriate acknowledgment in any
subsequent edition of this publication.

Concept Truck
Page 21

Mobile Crane
Page 14

Logging Truck
Page 8

Concrete Mixer Truck
Page 12

LeRoy Collins
Leon County Public Library
200 W. Park Avenue
Tallahassee, FL 32301

Mighty Machines

Big Rig

Caroline Bingham

Semitrailer
Page 6

Heavy Tow Truck
Page 16

Road Train
Page 18

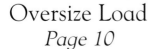

Oversize Load
Page 10

Semitrailer

A semitrailer has an engine that is more than four times as powerful as a standard road car's! It needs this power to pull heavy loads on long journeys. The semi, or rig, has two sections – a tractor unit and a trailer that can be separated from the tractor unit.

sleeping cabin

the front of a trailer links up to the tractor unit here

fuel to power the engine is stored in huge tanks

steps to driver's cab

  The **tractor unit** contains the driver's cab, the front driving wheels, and the engine.

some trucks are hand painted

trailer

Around the bend

The semi can bend where the trailer connects to the tractor unit so it is possible for it to turn corners.

sideview mirror

KENWORTH

AMAZING FACTS

Most tractor units contain a tiny bedroom. On overnight journeys, the driver pulls off the road to sleep.

In one year, a truck driver might easily cover 100,000 mi (160,000 km).

Some trucks have heated sideview mirrors to stop mist and ice from forming.

Logging Truck

A logging truck loads up with huge tree trunks at a tree felling site and takes them to a sawmill. The trunks are held in place on the open trailer by metal rods and are secured with cables.

all the branches are sawn off the trunk before the trunk is shipped

logs are piled high behind the driver's cab

metal rod

Trees are cut down at **tree felling sites**.

Grab and hold

Some logging trucks have built-in cranes, but often a separate crane machine will load the logs. The crane closes around the logs and grips them – just like you would pick up a handful of pencils.

the crane lifts when liquids are forced up these metal pipes

steel claws grip the logs

sideview mirror sticks out so driver can see past the logs

the engine is protected by a hood

the front wheels are covered by a wheel arch

all trucks have loud air horns

Oversize Load

Trucks sometimes have to carry strangely shaped loads, such as a boat, or even a house! This truck is carrying a wing for an airplane. It is very heavy and long, and the driver has to travel slowly. On public roads, a truck with an oversize load often has a police escort.

wing loaded onto trailer

this trailer is used to transfer the wing on airport grounds

wheels are joined together by an axle

 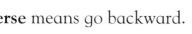

Remote control steering
The back of the trailer is steered around corners by remote control.

this trailer is used on public roads

when the load is secure, the driver will reverse to hitch the tractor unit to the trailer

G852 NDM

95 380 ATi

LEYLAND DAF

STGO CAT 2

bumper helps protect the truck if it is involved in an accident

AMAZING FACTS

This wing is as heavy as 525 seven-year-old children. But so many children would need a lot more space.

The loaded wing will clear highway bridges leaving a gap little bigger than the length of a banana. That's a tight fit!

When the wing is on the trailer on a public road, the rig is 125 ft (38 m) long. That's as long as 12 station wagons parked end to end.

Remote control gives an operator control from a distance.

Concrete Mixer Truck

AMAZING FACTS

🔩 A concrete mixer spins its load like a giant washing machine – it could wash 100 loads at once.

🔩 The inside of a concrete mixer's drum works by making the watery concrete mixture run uphill.

🔩 A concrete mixer is unstable because of the liquid sloshing around the drum.

🔩 6.5 tons (6 tonnes) of sand are used in each mixer load. You could build a 7 ft (2 m) high sandcastle with that.

If you see a concrete mixer on the road, you will probably see the drum turning around and around. It turns to mix its load and keep it from setting before the truck finishes its journey at a building site.

2527

2527

5687

M399 EFB

cab-over
tractor unit

🔩 In **cab-over** trucks the driver sits above the engine and front wheels. 🔩

Which way?
The drum turns one way to mix the concrete, and the other way to empty it.

mixed concrete leaves the drum along this chute

driver empties drum by remote control

drum

driver climbs the ladder to check the load

M399 EFB

2527

Redland Redland

Mobile Crane

Four huge metal legs called outriggers stretch out from this crane and find a firm position against the ground. The long crane arm, or jib, then reaches up into the air and the mobile crane is ready to lift.

Front view

feet, or jacks

outrigger

⊚ This crane can lift 550 tons (500 tonnes) – that's as much as 500 cars.

⊚ The crane has two engines – one to drive the machine, and one to operate the jib.

⊚ The crane's 18 wheels are all joined to the steering. When the crane turns, the back wheels turn at a different angle than the front wheels.

⊚ When the jib is up, a counter-weight has to balance the crane.

A **counterweight** is a heavy metal weight. It stops the crane from tipping over.

Fold up and go

Mobile cranes work on building and road construction sites, lifting heavy objects. When the operator wants to drive the crane to a new site, the jib pulls into itself like a telescope.

jib telescopes out from here

C 500

AINSCOUGH

INSCOUGH

M390

hook block is attached to cab when the crane is on the road

 The **jib** is a long metal arm. **Jacks** are big metal feet used to steady a machine. 15

Heavy Tow Truck

With its bright colors and flashing lights, this tow truck, or wrecker, is easy to spot at the scene of an accident. Once there, it slides a long piece of steel called an underlift under the damaged vehicle and tows it to a garage to be repaired.

a heat shield surrounds the exhaust pipe

sleeping cabin

underlift

tools are stored in this locker

truck has 62 sidelights

engine runs on diesel fuel, stored in two huge tanks

  Waste fumes leave the engine through the **exhaust pipe.**

Using spectacles

This tow truck has hooked a metal frame shaped like a pair of glasses under the front wheels of a tractor unit.

frame

emergency lights flash to warn people to keep clear of the truck

two side markers help the driver judge the width of the truck

FREIGHTLINER

URC 397X

ballast bumper

AMAZING FACTS

The ballast bumper weighs 1.5 tons (1.48 tonnes). That's as heavy as 11 baby elephants.

This truck can pull more than five times its own weight. Could you pull five of your friends?

Ballast acts as a counterwei   when the truck is towing a heavy vehicle.

Road Train

A road train pulls three or four trailers in the same way that a train pulls cars, but it travels on the road. Road trains only operate in Australia, where the distances between cities are so vast that long road trains are the best way to transport goods.

turn signal

radiator grille

TF·560
N.T. -NATURE TERRITORY-

ROAD

Turn signals flash yellow when the driver turns a corner or pulls over.

It bends like a snake

This road train is carrying fuel. Three trailer tanks are hitched together so it can bend if it needs to.

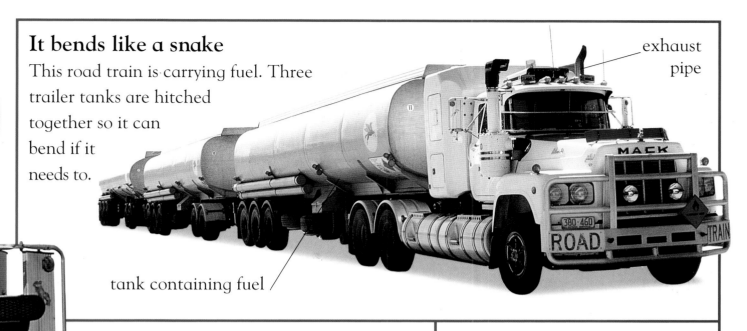

exhaust pipe

tank containing fuel

bug deflector helps keep the windshield clear of insects

air is sucked in and cleaned in this barrel. It mixes with the fuel to make the engine go

No entry

A road train cannot enter a city – it's too big! So the driver loads and unloads at special road train stations. A road train carries enough fuel to travel 2,200 mi (3,520 km).

FLAMMABLE LIQUID 3

road trains are marked so other drivers know the vehicle is unusually long

AMAZING FACTS

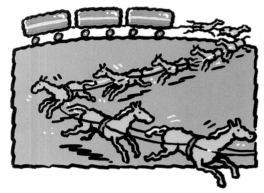

The most powerful road train has the pulling power of 600 horses.

You would have to link up with 414 friends to make a chain as long as the longest road train in the world – 1,244 ft (379 m).

 A **tank** is specially built to hold liquids.

Supertruck

A big rig has to push through lots of air as it moves along a road. If a manufacturer can cut down on the amount of air resistance, or drag, the truck will save fuel because the engine won't have to work as hard. The best way to do this is to make the truck a smoother shape – like this sleek new supertruck.

collar forces air up and over the back of the trailer

panels cover wheels to provide a flat surface against the air

Aerodynamic shapes are designed with rounded edges to slip through the air.

Concept truck

In trying to make trucks more aerodynamic in order to save fuel, truck designers sometimes develop ideas that look unusual. Just look at the shape of this truck!

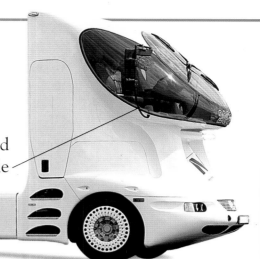

driver sits behind a glass bubble

Compared to older rigs, a supertruck saves about 50 soda cans worth of fuel every 60 mi (100 km). It would take a long time to get through that much soda.

This supertruck has only 12 wheels. Older model trucks may have up to 22 wheels.

This supertruck's cab is so tall that an adult can comfortably stand up inside it.

A **concept truck** is a truck that tries out a designer's new ideas.

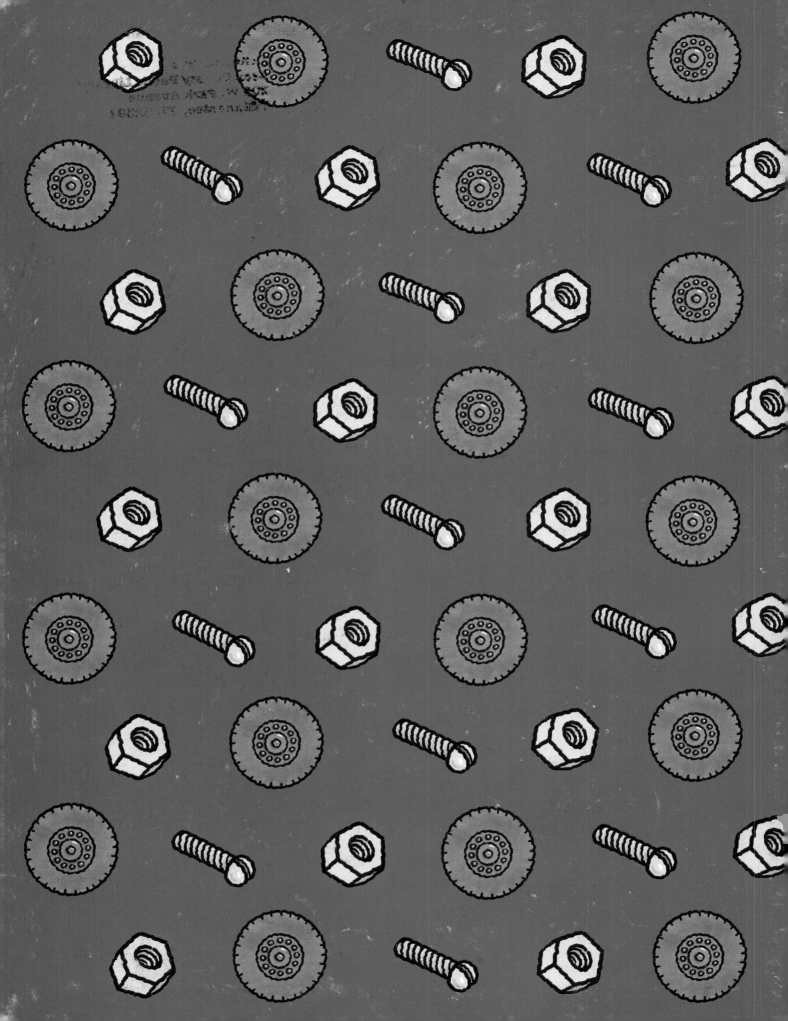